Learning about Cats

THE EXOTIC CAT

by Joanne Mattern

Consultant:
Johanna Leibfarth
Desmin Exotics
North Augusta, South Carolina

CAPSTONE
HIGH-INTEREST
BOOKS

an imprint of Capstone Press
Mankato, Minnesota

Capstone High-Interest Books are published by Capstone Press
151 Good Counsel Drive, P.O. Box 669, Mankato, Minnesota 56002
http://www.capstone-press.com

Library of Congress Cataloging-in-Publication Data
Mattern, Joanne, 1963–
    The Exotic cat/by Joanne Mattern.
    p. cm.—(Learning about cats)
    Includes bibliographical references and index (p. 48).
    ISBN 0-7368-0896-5
    I. Exotic shorthair cat—Juvenile literature. [1. Exotic shorthair cat. 2. Cats.
3. Pets.] I. Title. II. Series.
SF449.E93 M38 2002
636.8'2—dc21   00-013078

Summary: Discusses the history, development, habits, and care of Exotic cats.

Editorial Credits
Connie R. Colwell, editor; Lois Wallentine, product planning editor; Linda Clavel,
    cover designer and illustrator; Katy Kudela, photo researcher

Photo Credits
Carl J. Widmer, 20
Chanan Photography, 6, 16, 28, 39, 40–41
Delore Schwartz, 22, 26, 30, 34
Joan Balzarini, 33, 36
Larry Johnson, cover, 14, 18
Mark McCullough, 12
www.ronkimballstock.com, 4, 8, 10, 24

1 2 3 4 5 6 07 06 05 04 03 02

Table of Contents

Quick Facts about the Exotic 4

Chapter 1   The Exotic Cat 7

Chapter 2   Development of the Breed . . . 11

Chapter 3   Today's Exotic 17

Chapter 4   Owning an Exotic 21

Chapter 5   Caring for an Exotic 29

Photo Diagram 40

Quick Facts about Cats 42

Words to Know 44

To Learn More 45

Useful Addresses 46

Internet Sites 47

Index 48

Quick Facts about the Exotic

Description

Size: Exotic cats have short, sturdy bodies. They are medium-sized cats.

Weight: Adult Exotic cats weigh between 8 and 15 pounds (3.6 and 6.8 kilograms).

Physical features: The Exotic's plush coat is of medium length. Its head and eyes are large and round. Its nose is short and snub. The Exotic's body is round and stocky. Its legs are short and strong.

4

| **Colors:** | Exotics can be many colors. The most common colors are black, tortoiseshell, red tabby, brown tabby, and bi-color. A tortoiseshell Exotic has patches of black, red, and cream fur. Tabby Exotics have coats with darker striped markings. Bi-color Exotics have coats with patches of white and another color or pattern. |

Development

Place of origin:	The Exotic breed began in the United States.
History of breed:	Breeders developed the Exotic cat in the early 1960s. Breeders crossed Persian cats with American Shorthair cats to create the Exotic.
Numbers:	In 2000, the Cat Fanciers' Association (CFA) registered 2,094 Exotic cats. Owners who register their purebred cats record the cats' breeding records with an official organization. The CFA is the largest organization of cat breeders in the world.

Chapter 1

The Exotic Cat

The Exotic cat is a short, sturdy cat with a snub-nosed face. Some people call the Exotic "the teddy bear cat." They think these cats look like teddy bears.

The Exotic cat sometimes is called the Exotic Shorthair. Exotics look and behave a great deal like Persian cats. But Exotics have a short, plush coat. Persians have a long, thick coat.

Appearance

Exotics are medium-sized cats. Their bodies are stocky and low to the ground. They have short, sturdy legs. Their paws are large and round. Exotics' tails are short and thick.

Exotics have a short, plush coat. Their fur is thick and soft. It does not tangle or mat as

The Exotic sometimes is called "the teddy bear cat."

Many people think that Exotics have a sweet expression.

easily as the fur of a Persian cat. Like Persians, Exotic cats have a double coat. This coat has two layers. Thick, soft hair lies close to the skin. This thick layer of fur is covered by lighter, coarse fur.

Exotics have large eyes and a very short nose. Many people think that these features give the Exotic a sweet expression. Many Exotics have copper-colored eyes. Some white

Exotics have eyes of two different colors.
These colors often are green and blue.

Personality

Exotics are known for their calm and easygoing personalities. Exotics seem to enjoy being around people. They often follow their owners from room to room. But they do not demand attention.

Most Exotics make excellent pets. They are playful but gentle cats. They get along well with dogs, children, and other cats. Some breeders say male Exotics tend to be more affectionate than females.

Chapter 2

Development of the Breed

People developed the Exotic cat through careful breeding. They bred cats with the qualities they wanted in the Exotic breed.

The First Exotics

American Shorthair breeders developed the Exotic cat in the 1960s. American Shorthairs are medium-sized cats. Their short fur lies close to the skin. Some breeders of these cats wanted their cats to have silver coats. Some Persian cats had coats of this color. Breeders began crossing American Shorthairs with Persians.

Some of the resulting American Shorthair kittens had the desired silver coats. But they did not look like American Shorthairs. The kittens

Breeders used American Shorthairs to create the Exotic breed.

11

The Persian crosses led to cats that looked like Persians but had shorter coats.

had short, plush coats. Their faces looked like those of Persians.

Some breeders became interested in these unusual cats with short coats. Breeders began to cross Persians with other shorthaired cats such as Russian Blues and Burmese.

In 1966, the Cat Fanciers' Association (CFA) declared the new mixed-breed crosses a separate breed. This breed was called the Exotic Shorthair. Later, the name was changed to the Exotic.

Breeding and Genes

Exotic cats have short hair because of their genes. Genes are parts of the cells that carry information about how a living thing will look and behave. Genes determine a cat's coat, color, and gender. Kittens receive a pair of genes for each trait. They receive one gene from their mother and one gene from their father.

The gene for a shorthaired coat is dominant. Dominant genes are stronger than other genes. Cats with short coats need only one gene for short hair. Cats with one or both genes for short hair will be shorthaired.

These genes can make it difficult to breed Exotic cats. Exotic kittens sometimes inherit one gene for long hair from each parent. These kittens will have long hair. The kittens look like Persians. But they have Exotic parents.

Persians have double coats like Exotics do.

The longhaired kittens are registered as Exotics. But these cats cannot be exhibited as Exotics at CFA cat shows. They must compete in the Any Other Variety (AOV) category. Some cats that do not meet certain breed standards may compete in this class.

Other organizations allow longhaired Exotics to compete as a separate class. These organizations include the American Cat Fanciers' Association (ACFA) and the Cat Fanciers' Federation (CFF). The International Cat Association (TICA) allows longhaired Exotics to compete as Persians. Longhaired Exotics also can be used to breed Exotic kittens. They often are sold as pets.

Chapter 3

Today's Exotic

Today's Exotic cats look more like Persians than the Exotics of the past. Exotic breeders have worked to develop a cat that looks similar to the Persian. The only difference is the length of the Exotic's coat.

Breeders develop Exotics by crossing Persians with shorthaired cats. But breeders do this only once. The breeders then take the kittens from these matches and breed them with Persians. Today's Exotic kittens are almost entirely Persian. They are identical to Persians in appearance and personality. But Exotic kittens keep their shorter coats.

Today's Exotic is identical to the Persian in every way except for the length of the coat.

The breed standard says that Exotics should have short, snub noses.

Breed Standard

Judges look for certain physical features when they judge an Exotic in a cat show. These features are called the breed standard. The breed standard for the Exotic is almost the same as the breed standard for the Persian. The only difference is the description of the coat.

In general, an Exotic's body should be stocky and broad. Its legs should be short and sturdy. Its head should be large and round. Its eyes should be large and expressive. Its nose should be short and snub. Its tail should be short and thick.

An Exotic cat's coat should be medium-long, soft, and plush. The fur should not lie flat. Instead, it should stand out slightly from the cat's body.

Exotics can be many colors. The most common Exotic colors are black, tortoiseshell, red tabby, brown tabby, and bi-color. Tortoiseshell Exotics have patches of red, black, and cream fur. Tabby Exotics have dark, striped markings. Bi-color Exotics have coats with patches of white and another color or pattern. These colors and patterns include black, blue, cream, red, or tabby. Blue Exotics have blue-gray coats.

Chapter 4

Owning an Exotic

People who are interested in adopting an Exotic cat can do so in several ways. They may contact breeders, animal shelters, or breed rescue organizations.

Exotics from breeders can cost several hundred dollars. Animal shelters or rescue organizations can be less expensive places to adopt an Exotic cat. But these places rarely have Exotic cats.

Finding an Exotic through a Breeder

The best place to adopt an Exotic kitten is from a good breeder. Good breeders make sure their cats are healthy and meet the breed standard. People who buy a kitten from a breeder often can meet the kitten's parents.

The best place to adopt an Exotic is from a good breeder.

People who buy a kitten from a breeder often can meet the kitten's parents.

This meeting gives owners an idea of how the kitten will look and behave as an adult.

Many Exotic cat breeders live in the United States and Canada. People who want to find a local Exotic breeder can attend cat shows. Cat shows are good places to talk to cat breeders and see their cats.

Breeders sometimes advertise in newspapers and cat magazines. These ads are organized by breed. They list the names, addresses, and phone numbers of breeders. Some breeders have Internet sites.

People should visit breeders before they buy cats from them. People should get the medical history of the breeders' cats and check breeders' references. They can talk to people who have bought cats from the breeders. These people can describe their experiences with the breeders.

Animal Shelters

Many people adopt cats from animal shelters. These places try to find good homes for unwanted animals.

An animal shelter can be a good place to adopt a cat for several reasons. Owners who adopt a cat from an animal shelter may save the cat's life. Many more animals are brought to shelters than there are people available to adopt them. Animals that are not adopted may be euthanized. Shelter workers euthanize animals by injecting them with substances that stop their breathing or heartbeat.

Animal shelters usually have mixed-breed cats available for adoption.

Animal shelters also offer less expensive pets. Most shelters charge only a small fee. Some veterinarians provide discounts on medical services for shelter animals.

Shelters do have some disadvantages. Shelters often have mixed-breed pets available for adoption instead of purebred cats such as the Exotic. Shelters rarely have Exotic cats available. But people can contact a shelter. They can ask shelter workers to contact them if an Exotic cat is brought to the shelter.

Another difficulty with shelter animals is that their histories often are unknown. Shelter workers may have no information about their animals' parents, health, or behavior. Some owners may unknowingly adopt cats with medical or behavioral problems.

Breed Rescue Organizations

People interested in adopting a purebred Exotic cat may want to contact a breed rescue organization. Breed rescue organization members find unwanted or neglected animals. They care for the animals and try to find new owners to adopt them.

Breed rescue organizations are similar to animal shelters in many ways. But they usually rescue just one breed. They rarely euthanize the animals. Breed rescue organizations keep Exotics until people are available to adopt them.

Adopting an Exotic from a breed rescue organization can have some advantages over adopting from breeders and animal shelters.

Breed rescue organizations are less expensive than breeders. People may find a purebred Exotic for a small fee. These cats may even be registered.

People can find information about breed rescue organizations in several ways. Rescue organizations often have their own Internet sites. They also may advertise in newspapers or cat magazines. Animal shelters also may refer people to rescue organizations.

Breed rescue organizations may have Exotic cats available for adoption.

Caring for an Exotic

Exotics are strong, healthy cats. They can live
15 years or more with good care.

Indoor and Outdoor Cats

Some cat owners allow their cats to roam
outdoors. This practice is not safe. Cats that
roam outdoors are at a much greater risk for
diseases than cats that are kept indoors.
Outdoor cats also face dangers from cars and
other animals.

Owners of indoor cats need to provide
their cats with a litter box. Owners fill the
box with small bits of clay called litter. Cats
eliminate waste in litter boxes. Owners should
clean the waste out of the box each day and
change the litter often. Cats are clean animals.
They may refuse to use a dirty litter box.

Exotics are safest when kept indoors.

Dry food can help keep Exotic cats' teeth clean.

Both indoor and outdoor cats need to scratch. Cats mark their territories by leaving their scent on objects they scratch. Cats also scratch to release tension and to keep their claws sharp. This habit can be a problem if cats scratch on furniture, carpet, or curtains. Owners should provide their cats with scratching posts. Owners can buy scratching posts at pet stores. Cats seem to prefer scratching on sisal. This material is similar to rope. It is found on many scratching posts.

Feeding

Exotic cats need high-quality food. Most pet foods available in supermarkets or pet stores provide a balanced, healthy diet.

Some cat owners feed their cats dry food. This food usually is the least expensive type of cat food. It will not spoil if it is left in a dish. Dry food also can help keep cats' teeth clean.

Other owners feed their cats moist, canned food. This type of food should not be left out for more than one hour. It will spoil if it is left out for long periods of time. Owners who feed their cats moist food usually feed their adult cats twice each day. The amount of food needed depends on the individual cat.

Both types of food can be suitable for Exotic cats. Different cats may prefer different types of food. Owners can ask veterinarians for advice on which type of food is best for their cats.

Cats need to drink water to stay healthy. Owners should keep their cats' bowls filled with fresh, clean water. Owners should dump and refill water bowls each day. Owners should not give cats milk. Adult cats have trouble digesting milk.

Nail Care

The tip of a cat's claw is called the nail. Exotic cats need their nails trimmed each month. Trimming helps reduce damage if cats scratch on the carpet or furniture. It also protects cats from infections caused by ingrown nails. Infections can occur when a cat does not have an object for sharpening its nails. The nails then grow into the bottom of the paw.

It is best to begin trimming a cat's nails when it is a kitten. The kitten will become used to having its nails trimmed as it grows older. Veterinarians can show owners how to trim their cats' nails with a special nail clipper.

Dental Care

Exotic cats also need regular dental care to protect their teeth and gums from plaque. This coating of saliva and tiny organisms called

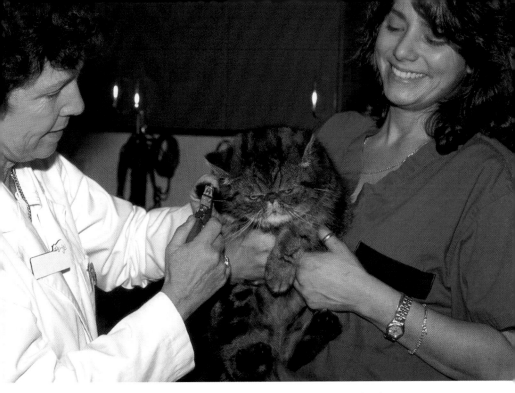

Veterinarians can show owners how to trim their cats' nails.

bacteria causes tooth decay and gum disease. Dry cat food helps remove plaque from cats' teeth. Owners also should brush their cats' teeth at least once per week. They can use a special toothbrush made for cats or a soft cloth. They should brush cats' teeth with toothpaste made for cats. Owners should never use toothpaste made for people to brush their cats' teeth. Cats may become sick if they swallow it.

Brushing may not be enough to remove the plaque from older cats' teeth. These cats may

Owners should comb their Exotics each week.

need a veterinarian to clean their teeth once each year.

Grooming

Most cats do a good job of grooming their fur with their tongues. But Exotics need help from their owners. Their coat grows very thick in winter. In late spring, Exotics begin to lose this thick coat. Owners should comb their Exotics with a fine-toothed metal comb each week. In spring and summer, Exotics should be combed more often. Combing helps remove loose hair. It also helps keep cats' coats shiny.

Owners should be gentle when combing Exotics. Combing can break off pieces of fur. It also can scrape cats' skin.

Combing prevents tangles of fur called mats. Owners should never use scissors to cut mats out of the coat. This practice could damage the cat's coat or cut its skin. Professional groomers should remove mats. These people are trained to bathe, comb, and brush animals.

Exotics sometimes develop dark stains around their eyes. Exotics' large eyes and flat faces allow tears to easily leak out of their eyes. The tears contain bacteria. The bacteria will stain Exotics' fur. Owners should clean around Exotics' eyes every day with a moistened tissue or cloth.

Health Problems

Most Exotic cats are healthy. But they sometimes can suffer from respiratory problems. Exotic cats' noses are short. This may cause breathing difficulties. Respiratory diseases can be treated with medicines called antibiotics.

Exotic cats must visit a veterinarian regularly for checkups.

Cats should be vaccinated to protect them from respiratory diseases. These shots of medicine help prevent serious diseases.

Exotic cats also can get hairballs. Cats lick themselves to groom their coats. They often swallow loose pieces of fur. This fur can form into balls in the cat's stomach. The only way the cat can get rid of these hairballs is to vomit them up. Large hairballs can get stuck in a cat's digestive system. Surgery may be needed to remove them.

Combing an Exotic regularly is the best way to prevent hairballs. Combing removes loose fur before the cat can swallow it. Medicines also are available that prevent hairballs. These medicines contain petroleum jelly. The jelly coats hairballs in the cat's stomach. The coating helps them pass harmlessly in the cat's waste.

Cats sometimes get diseases that are passed down from their parents. Good cat breeders test their animals for these diseases. They will not breed animals that suffer from serious illnesses. Breeders should have information on their cats' medical histories. This information is important when choosing an Exotic cat.

Veterinarian Visits

Exotic cats must visit a veterinarian regularly for checkups. Most veterinarians recommend yearly visits for cats. Older cats may need to visit the veterinarian two or three times each year. Cats tend to have more health problems as they get older. More frequent checkups help veterinarians treat these health problems.

An owner who adopts an Exotic cat should make a checkup appointment as soon as possible.

The veterinarian will check the cat's heart, lungs, internal organs, eyes, ears, mouth, and coat.

The veterinarian also will vaccinate the cat against diseases. These diseases include rabies, feline panleukopenia, and feline leukemia.

Rabies is spread by animal bites. This disease can be deadly. Feline panleukopenia also is called feline distemper. This virus causes fever, vomiting, and death. Cats also can be vaccinated against several respiratory diseases that cause breathing or lung problems. These diseases include the rhinostracheitis virus, the calici virus, and chlamydia psittaci.

Owners who bring their cats to cat shows often vaccinate them for feline leukemia. This disease attacks a cat's immune system. It leaves the cat unable to fight off infections and other illnesses. Feline leukemia is spread from cat to cat by bodily fluids.

Cats receive some vaccinations each year and others less often. Breeders have information on which vaccinations Exotic cats need.

Veterinarians also spay female cats and neuter male cats. These surgeries make it impossible for cats to breed. Owners who are

Exotics need some vaccinations each year.

not planning to breed their cats should have them spayed or neutered. These surgeries keep unwanted kittens from being born. They also help prevent infections and diseases such as cancers of the reproductive organs. Spayed and neutered cats usually have calmer personalities than cats that are not spayed or neutered. They also are unlikely to wander away from home to find mates.

Exotic cats make excellent pets for many people. Owners enjoy the easygoing personalities and appearance of these "teddy bear cats."

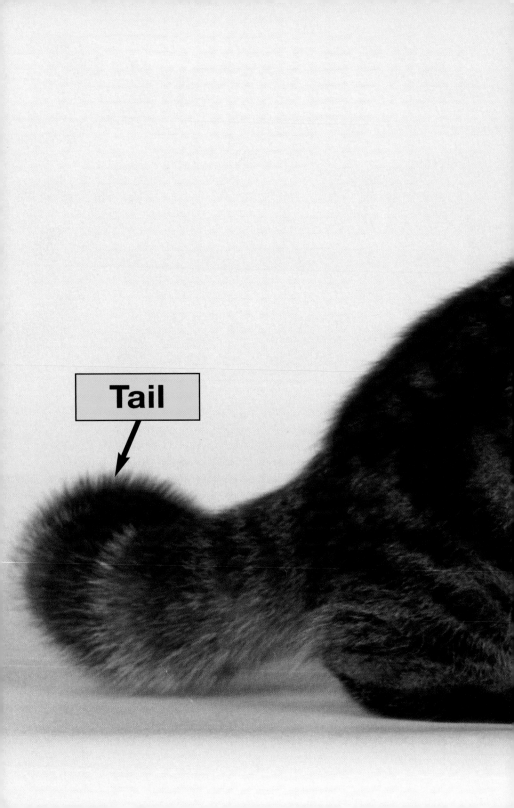

Tail

Ears

Whiskers

Paws

Quick Facts about Cats

A male cat is called a tom. A female cat is called a queen. A young cat is called a kitten. A family of kittens born at one time is called a litter.

Origin: Shorthaired cat breeds descended from a type of African wildcat called *Felis lybica*. Longhaired breeds may have descended from Asian wildcats. People domesticated or tamed these breeds as early as 1500 B.C.

Types: The Cat Fanciers' Association accepts 40 domestic cat breeds for competition. The smallest breeds weigh about 5 to 7 pounds (2.3 to 3.2 kilograms) when grown. The largest breeds can weigh more than 18 pounds (8.2 kilograms). Cat breeds may be either shorthaired or longhaired. Cats' coats can be a variety of colors. These colors include many shades of white, black, gray, brown, and red.

Reproduction: Most cats are sexually mature at 5 or 6 months. A sexually mature female cat goes into estrus several times each year. Estrus also is called "heat." During this time, she can mate with a male. Kittens are born about 65 days after breeding. An average litter includes four kittens.

Development: Kittens are born blind and deaf. Their eyes open about 10 days after birth. Their hearing develops at the same time. They can live on their own when they are 6 weeks old.

Life span: With good care, cats can live 15 or more years.

Sight: A cat's eyesight is adapted for hunting. Cats are good judges of distance. They see movement more easily than detail. Cats also have excellent night vision.

Hearing: Cats can hear sounds that are too high for humans to hear. A cat can turn its ears to focus on different sounds.

Smell: A cat has an excellent sense of smell. Cats use scents to establish their territories. Cats scratch or rub the sides of their faces against objects. These actions release a scent from glands between their toes or in their skin.

Taste: Cats cannot taste as many foods as people can. For example, cats are not very sensitive to sweet tastes.

Touch: Cats' whiskers are sensitive to touch. Cats use their whiskers to touch objects and sense changes in their surroundings.

Balance: Cats have an excellent sense of balance. They use their tails to help keep their balance. Cats can walk on narrow objects without falling. They usually can right themselves and land on their feet during falls from short distances.

Communication: Cats use many sounds to communicate with people and other animals. They may meow when hungry or hiss when afraid. Cats also purr. Scientists do not know exactly what causes cats to make this sound. Cats often purr when they are relaxed. But they also may purr when they are sick or in pain.

Words to Know

breeder (BREED-ur)—someone who breeds and raises cats or other animals

breed standard (BREED STAN-durd)—certain physical features in a breed that judges look for in a breed at a cat show

double coat (DUH-buhl KOHT)—a coat that is thick and soft close to the skin and covered with lighter, silky fur on the surface

estrus (ESS-truss)—a physical state of a female cat during which she will mate with a male cat; estrus also is known as "heat."

euthanize (YOO-thuh-nize)—to painlessly put an animal to death by injecting it with a substance that stops its breathing or heartbeat

mat (MAT)—a thick, tangled mass of hair

neuter (NOO-tur)—to remove a male animal's testicles so that it cannot reproduce

spay (SPAY)—to remove a female animal's uterus and ovaries so that it cannot reproduce

vaccination (vak-suh-NAY-shun)—a shot of medicine that protects a person or animal from disease

To Learn More

Commings, Karen. *Guide to Owning an Exotic Shorthair.* Popular Cat Library. Philadelphia: Chelsea House, 1999.

Davis, Karen Leigh. *The Exotic Shorthair Cat: Everything about Acquisition, Care, Nutrition, Behavior, Health Care, and Breeding.* Hauppauge, N.Y.: Barron's Educational Series, 1997.

Petras, Kathryn, and Ross Petras. *Cats: 47 Favorite Breeds, Appearance, History, Personality, and Lore.* Fandex Family Field Guides. New York: Workman Publishing, 1997.

You can read articles about Exotic cats in *Cat Fancy* and *Cats* magazines.

Useful Addresses

Canadian Cat Association (CCA)
289 Rutherford Road South
Unit 18
Brampton, ON L6W 3R9
Canada

Cat Fanciers' Association (CFA)
P.O. Box 1005
Manasquan, NJ 08736-0805

The International Cat Association (TICA)
P.O. Box 2684
Harlingen, TX 78551

Internet Sites

American Cat Fanciers Association (ACFA)
http://www.acfacat.com

American Veterinary Medical Association Presents: Care for Pets
http://www.avma.org/care4pets

Canadian Cat Association (CCA)
http://www.cca-afc.com

Cat Fanciers
http://www.fanciers.com

Cat Fanciers' Association (CFA)
http://www.cfainc.org

Cats Online
http://www.cats.org.uk

Fanciers Breeder Referral List (FBRL)
http://www.breedlist.com

Index

American Shorthairs, 11–12

animal shelters, 21, 23–25, 27

breeder, 9, 11, 12, 17, 21–23, 25, 27, 37, 38

breed rescue organizations, 21, 25, 27

breed standard, 14, 18–19, 21

Burmese, 12

coat, 7–8, 11–12, 13, 17, 18, 19, 34–35, 36, 38

color, 9, 11, 13, 19

dental care, 32–34

feeding, 31–32

genes, 13

grooming, 34–35

hairballs, 36–37

litter box, 29

Persians, 7, 8, 11, 12, 13, 15, 17, 18

personalities, 9, 17, 39

Russian Blues, 12

scratching, 30–31

vaccinations, 36, 38

veterinarian, 24, 31, 32, 34, 37–38